Table of Contents

Puzzle Group Assignment

Materials:

- Assorted border strips
- Scissors
- Paper bag

Directions:

1. Puzzle-cut each border into as many pieces as there will be members in the group.
2. Place all of the pieces in a bag.
3. Let each student choose a piece.
4. Instruct students to quietly walk around the classroom, trying to find their group members by matching up the border puzzle pieces.

Hall Passes

Materials:

- Assorted border strips
- Scissors
- Markers
- Laminating machine
- Hole punch
- Shoelaces or other string

Directions:

1. Cut borders into 6" sections.
2. Write the purpose of the hall pass on the back of each border section. Examples include: *Boys, Girls, Office, Library, Messenger, Nurse.*
3. Laminate the sections and trim off excess.
4. Punch a hole in the end of each hall pass.
5. Thread a shoelace through the hole and tie the ends together.
6. Let students wear the hall passes as necklaces when leaving the classroom without supervision.

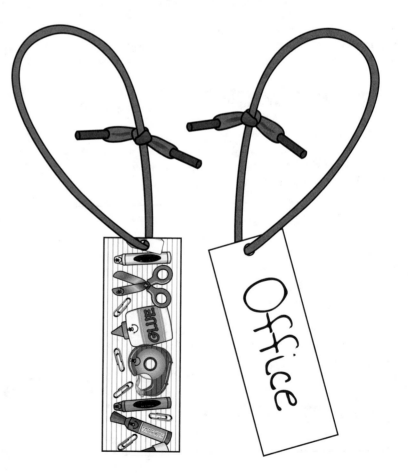

Work Toppers

Materials:

- Assorted border strips
- Student papers
- Permanent markers
- Stapler

Directions:

1. Display student papers on a bulletin board.
2. Cut border strips into 12" sections.
3. Write student names or positive words, such as *Great!, Fantastic!,* or *Super Work!* on border sections.
4. Staple a border section above each student paper.

Floor Plans

Materials:

- Straight border strips
- Clear, wide packaging tape

Directions:

1. Plot out an area of the classroom to section off for a specific purpose, such as a center, a reading nook, or an area to sit in during morning calendar.
2. Place border strips on the floor to delineate the area.
3. Tape the border securely to the floor.

Computer Helper

Materials:
- Assorted border strips
- Scissors
- Tape

Directions:
1. Cut border to fit around class computer screens.
2. Secure with tape.
3. Let students write addresses of fun and interesting web sites they visit on the border.
4. Change the border with seasons or curriculum themes.

Calendar Cover-Ups

Materials:
- Straight seasonal and holiday border strips
- Scissors
- Permanent marker
- Tape
- Calendar Grid

Directions:
1. Cut border into squares.
2. Use a marker to write numbers 1-31 on the squares.
3. Each day, tape a square to the calendar grid.
4. Make a set of squares for each month, and special squares for birthdays, holidays, and special events.

SEPTEMBER

Sunday	Monday	Tuesday	Wednesday	Thursday	Friday	Saturday
					1	2
3	4	5	6	7	8	9
10	11	12	13	14	15	16
17	18	19	20	21	22	23
24	25	26	27	28	29	30

Bookmarks

Materials:
- Assorted straight border strips
- Hole punch
- Colorful yarn
- Scissors

Directions:
1. Cut border into 8" sections.
2. Punch a hole in one end of each section.
3. Cut a long length of yarn, double it, and thread it through the hole.
4. Tie a knot as close as possible to the top edge of the border, forming a loop with a 2"-3" tail.
5. Cut the loop and trim the yarns to equal lengths.
6. If desired, write a special message on the back, or use to keep track of books read.

Award Bracelets

Materials:
- Assorted border strips
- Permanent marker
- Stapler
- Scissors

Directions:
1. Cut 8"-9" strips of border.
2. If desired, write award messages on the border strips.
3. To reward a student, staple the border strip around his wrist, like a bracelet.
4. Let him wear his award bracelet all day, then wear it home to share with his family.

Shelf and Mailbox Labels

Materials:
- Assorted border strips
- Permanent markers
- Tape

Directions:
1. Tape border along the edges of shelves, cubbies, or student mailboxes, so that it extends below the shelf.
2. Label the border with what should be stored on particular shelves, student names, etc.

Pocket Folders

Materials:
- 12" x 18" construction paper, assorted colors
- Assorted straight border strips
- Tape
- Scissors

Directions:
1. Cut a strip of border the same length as a sheet of construction paper.
2. Place the border along the bottom of the paper. Tape along the bottom and side edges of the border, folding the tape under to secure the border to the paper.
3. Fold the paper in half, like a book, with the border on the inside.
4. Cut out figures and designs from matching border scraps and glue them to the front of the folder for decoration.

Height Chart

Materials:
- 2-3 simple scalloped border strips
- Ruler
- Scissors
- Permanent marker
- Tape

Directions:
1. Orient a strip of border horizontally so the scalloped edge is along the top.
2. Using a ruler, check to be sure that the tops of the scallops are 2" apart.
3. Cut the right end of the border through the middle of the last scallop.
4. Orient the strip vertically so the scalloped edge is on the right side.
5. Starting with the number 2 on the first whole scallop, write even numbers in each scallop.
6. Mark in the middle of each dip between scallops to represent odd numbers.
7. Tape the border to a wall.
8. Matching up the scallops, add more border and fill in the numbers.
9. Let students stand beside the height chart to see how tall they are!

Borders

Awards and Coupons

Materials:

- Assorted bulletin board accents with writing space
- Permanent marker

Directions:

1. Write positive messages and rewards on each bulletin board accent. Examples include: *No homework tonight, Sit with a friend, Keep up the good work,* and *Thanks for lending a hand.*
2. Give coupons and awards to students as incentives for good work and behavior.

Name Tags

Materials:

- Assorted bulletin board accents
- Permanent marker
- Heavy duty tape
- Safety pins

Directions:

1. Write student names on bulletin board accents.
2. If desired, laminate for durability.
3. Tape a safety pin to the back of each accent.
4. Carefully pin name tags to students' shirts for the first day of school, on field trips, or to help substitutes.

8

Pencil Topper

Materials:
- Bulletin board accents
- Craft knife
- Pencils or lollipops

Directions:
1. Using a craft knife, cut two 1" slits in the accent about 2" apart.
2. Slide a pencil or lollipop through the slits.
3. If desired, write a message on the accent piece.
4. Give to students on the first day of school, as rewards, or as party favors.

Bookmarks

Materials:
- Assorted bulletin board accents
- Craft knife

Directions:
1. With a craft knife, carefully cut a half-circle shape near the top of the accent.
2. To mark a page, pop out the cut area and slip it over the pages.
3. Give students different bookmarks to keep their places in each of their textbooks and reading books.

Decorative Border

Materials:

- Coordinating bulletin board accents
- Tape or stapler

Directions:

1. Alternating accents, create a pattern around the border of a bulletin board.
2. Staple or tape to secure the border.
3. If desired, make the border interactive by writing rewards or assignments on each accent and letting students choose daily from the border. You may also allow students to write accomplishments, such as books read, facts learned, or kind words, on accent pieces.

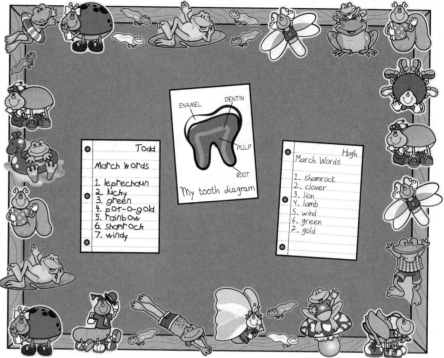

Fancy Letters

Materials:

- Coordinating bulletin board accents
- Permanent markers

Directions:

1. Write each letter of a bulletin board title on an accent.
2. Display the accents together to form a colorful title.
3. Use the letters to make titles stand out on bulletin boards, center signs, door displays, etc.

10

Large Letters

Materials:

- Matching bulletin board accents
- Tape or stapler

Directions:

1. Arrange accents on a bulletin board or wall to form large letters.
2. Staple or tape to secure.
3. If desired, attach accents to sentence strips to form large letters to make the letters easier to reuse.

Clock Helpers

Materials:

- 12 matching bulletin board accents with open writing space
- Permanent marker
- Masking tape
- 4 additional matching accents (optional)

Directions:

1. On each accent, write the last two numbers of a digital clock time for each number on the clock. For example, for 12 write ":00," for 1 write ":05," etc.
2. Tape each accent to the wall around the clock beside its number.
3. Additional accents can be added beside these to note *quarter after*, *half past*, and *quarter till*.
4. Students can refer to these clock helpers and easily say what time it is!

Partner Assignment

Materials:

- Assorted bulletin board accents
- Permanent marker
- Bag or box

Directions:

1. Write each student's name on an accent piece.
2. Place accents in a bag or box.
3. Have students draw names to determine their partners on a project. (Remember, only half the students will pick a name.)

Student Work Placards

Materials:

- Assorted bulletin board accents with writing space
- Permanent marker

Directions:

1. Choose an accent piece for each student and write his name, grade, and teacher.
2. Laminate the accent pieces.
3. Tape an accent piece to the corner of student papers to highlight the artist, author, mathematician, etc., when displaying work in the halls and other common areas.

Discipline Cards

Materials:

- 3-4 matching bulletin board accents for each student (each of the four accents should be a different color, and each student should have the same set of four colors)
- 4 more of the same accents
- Marker
- Poster board
- Paper pocket or self-sticking hooks

Directions:

1. Place the same four accents (one of each color) in a paper pocket on a bulletin board for each student, or punch holes at the tops of the accents and hang them on hooks.
2. Write each student's name on his pocket or above his hook.
3. Glue the four additional accents along the left side of the poster board.
4. Beside each accent, write what it means. For example, a blue pencil means no problems, a yellow pencil is a warning, a green pencil is time out and a note home, and a red pencil means a call home.
5. Display the poster on the board with the pockets.
6. Each morning, arrange each student's accents in order with the "no problems" accent on top.
7. Throughout the day, if a student misbehaves, have him arrange his cards so the next card is showing. At the end of the day, you can easily see how each child acted and which parents should be contacted.

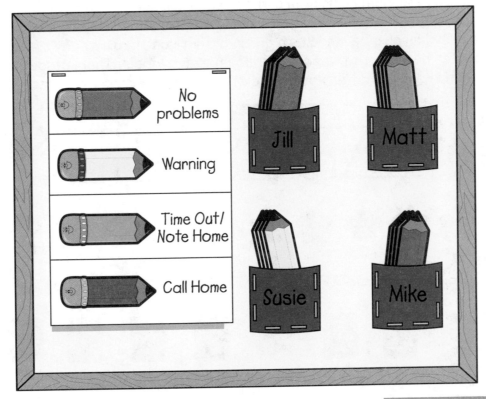

Desk Reference Name Plates

Materials:

- 2 handprint stickers (left and right)
- Stickers in pink, red, orange, yellow, green, blue, purple, brown
- 10 stickers with a simple design (dots, stars, etc.)
- 12"x 6" piece of poster board
- Pen or marker
- Permanent marker
- Clear, wide packaging tape

Directions:

1. Place the handprint stickers in the top left and right corners of the poster board. With a pen, label the stickers *left* and *right*.
2. Draw handwriting lines between the handprint stickers. Make the distance between the baseline and top line about 1" and draw the dashed center line between them. Using a colored marker, write a child's first and last names on the lines.
3. Under the handwriting line, place the ten simple stickers side by side.
4. Using a permanent marker, write the numbers 1-10 on the stickers. Then, using a pen, write the corresponding number word under each sticker.
5. Under the numbers, draw another row of handwriting lines, making the distance between baseline and top line ¹/₂". Write the alphabet on these lines. (Another option is to use blank handwriting line desk tape.)
6. Under the alphabet, place the color stickers in rainbow order across the bottom. With a pen, write the corresponding color word under each sticker.
7. Prepare the desk reference name plates before students arrive and tape them securely to their desks. They can also be made as a group activity on the first day of school by preparing the poster board with the handwriting lines and labels. Then, students can write their names and the alphabet and place the stickers in the correct places.

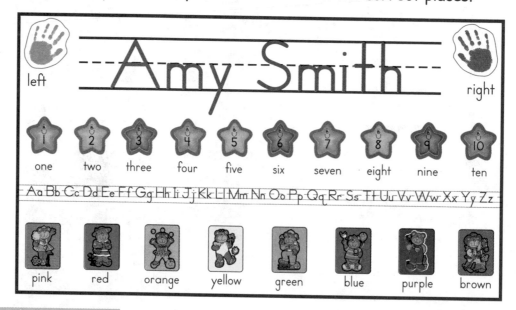

Track 100 Days of School

Materials:
- Assorted thematic stickers
- Sentence strips
- Marker

Directions:
1. Choose stickers to match seasonal themes, such as apples, pumpkins, mittens, and flowers.
2. Each school day, number a sticker and attach it, in order, to a sentence strip. Post the sentence strips in sequential order.
3. On the 100th day of school, attach a star sticker to the strip and decorate the surrounding area with markers.

Mark Group Supplies

Materials:
- Assorted stickers (one for each table or work group)

Directions:
1. Choose a different sticker for each table or group of students in the class.
2. Attach a sticker to items each group will be using throughout the year, such as glue bottles, markers, or crayons. Students can return the supplies they use to the appropriate containers.

Stickers

Sticker Booklets

Materials:

- Assorted stickers
- Several sheets of white paper
- Stapler
- Markers or pens

Directions:

1. Have students make small booklets by cutting and stapling together several sheets of paper.
2. Label each page with a month of the year.
3. Have students attach the stickers they receive throughout the school year on the appropriate pages in their booklets.

Class Scrapbook

Materials:

- Assorted stickers
- Photo albums or scrapbooks
- Photographs or drawings of school events
- Markers

Directions:

1. Group photographs or drawings of different events throughout the school year and place them on separate pages in a photo album or scrapbook.
2. Provide stickers and allow students to decorate the pages. Let students add their own designs using markers.
3. Students can make their own photo albums using miniature photo albums and assorted stickers. Students can also add the date and activity underneath their pictures.

Cubby or Locker Tags

Materials:
- Large shaped note pads
- Permanent marker
- Clear, self-adhesive paper

Directions:
1. Using a permanent marker, label a note pad with the name of each student in the class.
2. Attach the name tag to each student's cubby or locker by covering it with a piece of clear, self-adhesive paper.

Job Assignment

Materials:
- Matching small and large note pads
- Marker

Directions:
1. Write classroom jobs such as *Line Leader* or *Messenger* on large sheets of note pad paper. Laminate if desired.
2. Write student names on sheets of small note pad paper.
3. Post the classroom jobs on a wall or bulletin board display. Place a student name beside the job he or she is assigned to do.

Student Incentive Charts

Materials:

- Large note pad
- Ruler
- Marker
- Small stickers or chart seals

Directions:

1. Draw a grid in the center of a large note pad.
2. Write the student's name at the top of the grid.
3. Attach chart seals to the grid to reward or recognize good work.

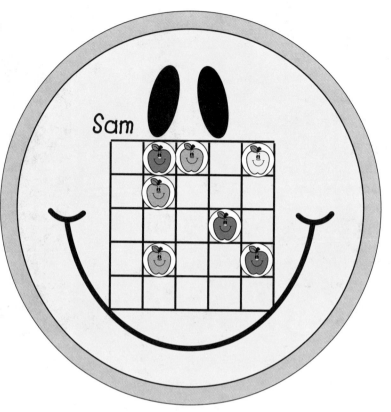

Calendar Cover-Ups

Materials:

- Small seasonal or holiday self-sticking note pads
- Calendar
- Marker

Directions:

1. Label the appropriate number of note pad sheets with the dates of a specific month.
2. Each day, attach the note pad to denote the date on the class calendar.
3. You may want to mark special events such as birthdays or graduation using theme-related note pads.

March

Sunday	Monday	Tuesday	Wednesday	Thursday	Friday	Saturday
					1	2
3	4	5	6	7	8	9
10	11	12	13	14	15	16
17	18	19	20	21	22	23
24	25	26	27	28	29	30
31						

18

Reward Tree

Materials:

- Apple or leaf-shaped note pads
- Brown and green construction paper
- Marker

Directions:

1. Cut out a large tree shape from brown and green paper. Size it to fit on a bulletin board or wall.
2. Write incentives or rewards such as *15 Minutes of Free Time* or *No Homework* on sheets of note pad paper. Attach the sheets to the tree.
3. Reward students for good behavior or outstanding work by letting them choose a reward from the tree.
4. You may want to adapt the tree for Open House by posting supplies needed on the display. Let parents and volunteers take off the note pad pages listing the supplies they will provide.

Kind Messages

Materials:

- Note pad
- Pencil

Directions:

1. Designate a small section of a bulletin board or wall for "kind messages."
2. Attach a note pad and pencil to the board. Allow students to write and post kind messages about each other, such as *Sam was nice to help me with math.*
3. After several weeks, collect the messages and let the recipients take them home to share.

19

Matching Games

Materials:
- Large and small note pad with the same theme
- Marker

Directions:
1. Choose a skill such as abbreviations for days of the week or math facts. Program sheets from the large note pad with a word or problem.
2. Program sheets from the small note pad with problem answers.
3. Post the large note pads on a bulletin board.
4. Have students attach the answers to the problems using push pins.
5. If desired, create a board game by gluing the large note pads to a piece of poster board. Laminate the board for durability.

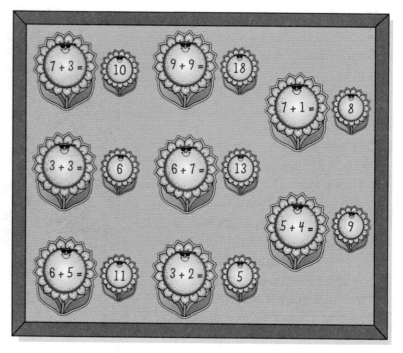

Talking Characters

Materials:
- Animal or character note pads
- White paper
- Scissors
- Markers

Directions:
1. Choose a character or animal note pad. Create a speech balloon by cutting out a circle from white paper.
2. Write activity directions or announcements in the speech balloon.
3. Post the note pad and the speech balloon on a wall or bulletin board.

20

"Happy-Gram" Necklaces

Materials:
- Large note pad
- Yarn
- Hole punch
- Marker

Directions:
1. Write happy or positive messages on a large note pad sheet to recognize outstanding student work or behavior.
2. Punch a hole in the top of the note pad and thread yarn through the hole. Tie the ends together.
3. Let students wear their special "happy- grams" as necklaces.

Work Reminders

Materials:
- Large note pad
- Assorted chart seals or foil star stickers
- Marker

Directions:
1. Each week, label a note pad sheet with a student's name and the date.
2. Post weekly assignments on the chalkboard, numbering each one.
3. Let students write each number on the note pad.
4. When a student completes an assignment, have him put a sticker on the number.
5. At the end of the week, reward students who have completed all their assignments.

Name Plates

Materials:
- Punch-out letters
- Clear packing tape
- Stickers

Directions:
1. Tape each student's name or initials on his desktop using punch-out letters and clear packing tape.
2. When students demonstrate good behavior, give them stickers to attach to their names.
3. When the name tags are filled with stickers, peel them off the desks. Attach a second piece of tape to the backs and let students bring the tags home.

Build a Phrase

Materials:
- Punch-out letters
- Tape

Directions:
1. Choose a positive phrase, such as *Excellent Work* or *Great Job*.
2. Post the phrase on the bulletin board. Reward students by posting a letter of the phrase underneath the completed phrase each time they demonstrate good behavior.
3. When the phrase is completed, reward students with a special treat.

Crowns

Materials:
- Assorted scalloped border
- Staples
- Glue
- Feathers, buttons, glitter, etc.
- Scissors

Directions:
1. Measure and cut a strip of border to fit snugly around a child's head.
2. Staple to secure.
3. Glue on various decorations.
4. Let children wear their crowns for special occasions, such as birthdays, graduation, parties, student of the week, etc.

Game Board Pieces

Materials:
- Short scalloped border scraps
- Scissors
- Tape

Directions:
1. Bend a border scrap into a cylinder, overlapping the back so that there is one crest in the front and one crest in the back.
2. Trim off excess border.
3. Tape border to secure the cylinder.
4. Stand the cylinder to move along a game board path.
5. Use to replace lost game pieces or create your own game.

Glasses or Masks

Materials:

- 15" scalloped border strips (be sure that a valley in the scallop pattern occurs in the center of the strip to rest on a student's nose)
- Scissors
- Ruler
- Glue
- Feathers, glitter, buttons, etc.

Directions:

1. Orient the border strip horizontally so that the scalloped edge is along the bottom.
2. Fold the border $4\frac{1}{2}$" from each end.
3. Leaving a $1\frac{1}{2}$" space in the middle, cut two eyeholes in the center section.
4. Decorate as desired.
5. To wear glasses, place the valley on the bridge of your nose and place the sides over your ears.

Small Cards

Materials:

- Assorted border strips
- Marker
- Scissors
- Ribbon or tape

Directions:

1. Cut off a section of border and fold like a card, so a complete design shows on the front.
2. Use a marker to write a message inside the card.
3. Tape the card on a package, or punch a hole in the corner and tie to a ribbon.

Frames

Materials:
- Assorted border strips
- Scissors
- Tape

Directions:
1. Tape border around all sides of a photo, work of art, or writing sample to display on a wall.
2. Use themed borders to accent the subject in the photo, drawing, or writing.
3. Turn scalloped borders in or out for different effects.

Finger Puppets

Materials:
- Border strips with characters
- Scissors
- Tape

Directions:
1. Cut apart the characters on the border.
2. Cut a $1/2$" wide border strip.
3. Tape the strip to the back of a character so the strip forms a finger-sized loop.
4. Slide the loop over a finger and use the finger puppet to act out stories, songs, plays, etc.

back view

Dominoes

Materials:
- Straight border strips with a repeating pattern of 5 or more items
- Scissors

Directions:
1. Cut border strips into sections that each include two items from the pattern (dominoes). Try not to include the same two items on more than 1 or 2 dominoes. (If there are single items left over from the border, tape them together to form complete dominoes.)
2. Give each child 10 dominoes.
3. In pairs, let the children take turns laying dominoes, so the item on the end of a domino matches the item on the end of the domino next to it.
4. If a child does not have a domino that matches any open end, he loses a turn.
5. The first child to place all of his dominoes wins.

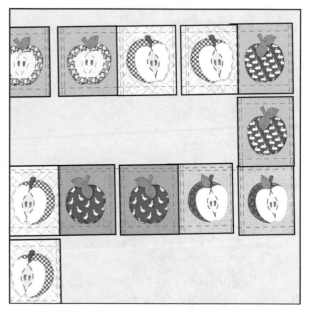

(Sample Domino game)

26

Magnets

Materials:
- Assorted bulletin board accents
- Magnetic tape

Directions:
1. Cut 2" sections of magnetic tape.
2. Affix the magnetic tape to the backs of bulletin board accents so the accents will adhere to metallic surfaces like lockers, refrigerators, etc.
3. If desired, write positive words and phrases on the accents and use the magnets to hold excellent papers!

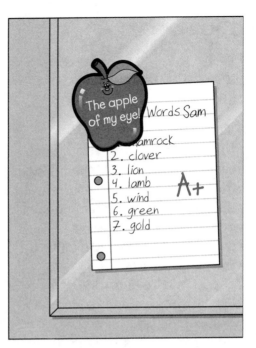

Garland

Materials:
- 12 bulletin board accent pieces
- 3 paper fasteners
- Hole punch
- Glue

Directions:
1. Arrange accent pieces, side by side, in groups of three. Overlap the edges.
2. Glue the sections together to form four long pieces.
3. Punch a hole in both sides of each piece.
4. Connect the pieces, matching holes and securing with paper fasteners.
5. Make as many sets as desired and attach together.
6. Hang garland around bulletin boards, under the chalkboard ledge, across the teacher's desk, along the walls near the ceiling, etc.

Question Cards

Materials:
- Assorted bulletin board accents
- Markers

Directions:
1. Write questions (math problems, review questions, story comprehension questions, etc.) and the answers on the backs of 20-30 bulletin board accents.
2. Place the cards text-side down between two students.
3. Let each child take a turn drawing a card from the pile and asking her partner the question.
4. If her partner gets the answer correct, the partner keeps the card. If her partner answers incorrectly, the card is put at the bottom of the pile.
5. The winner is the child with the most cards at the end of the game.

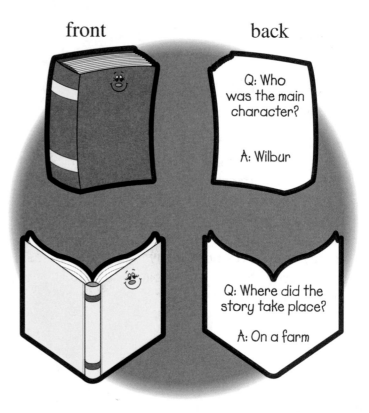

front   back

Q: Who was the main character?

A: Wilbur

Q: Where did the story take place?

A: On a farm

Puzzles

Materials:
- Assorted bulletin board accents
- Pencil
- Scissors
- Resealable plastic bags

Directions:
1. Using a pencil, lightly draw puzzle patterns on the backs of the accent pieces.
2. Carefully cut out the pieces along the lines drawn.
3. Place each puzzle in a resealable bag for easy storage.

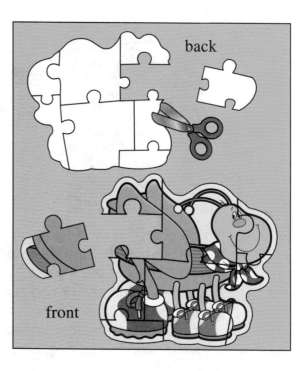

back

front

Lacing Cards

Materials:
- Assorted bulletin board accents
- Hole punch
- Shoelaces or yarn
- Masking tape

Directions:
1. Punch holes, about an inch apart, around the edges of bulletin board accents.
2. Give each student a shoelace and a punched accent and have her lace the shoelace through the holes.
3. If shoelaces are not available, wrap masking tape around both ends of a three-foot length of yarn to prevent fraying while lacing.

Poke Cards

Materials:
- Assorted bulletin board accents with writing space
- Permanent marker
- Green marker
- Hole punch
- Pencils

Directions:
1. Write a question at the top of a bulletin board accent.
2. Punch two holes at the bottom of the accent and write an answer below each hole (one correct and one incorrect).
3. Draw a green circle on the back of the card around the hole of the correct answer.
4. Place pencils and several cards with related questions at a center.
5. Students should poke the tip of a pencil through the card to choose the answer, then turn the card over to check the answer.

front

$5 \times 2 =$

10   7

back

Balancing Game

Materials:

- 5 sets of 10 of the same bulletin board accents
- Permanent marker
- Clear packing tape
- Bag

Directions:

1. Tape 5 accents from each set to the floor in a regular grid pattern that is 5" x 5".
2. On the remaining accents, write one of the following: *left foot, right foot, left hand, right hand.* Place the accents in a bag.
3. Let five students play at a time. Have one student draw cards for the other four. If the drawer pulls a red apple, for example, with the words *right hand* on it, one student puts her right hand on a red apple on the floor.
4. Let the drawer continue drawing accents and having students change their positions on the grid.
5. If a student loses her balance, she is out. The last student remaining wins.

Puppets

Materials:

- Bulletin board accents that are characters
- Craft sticks
- Tape
- Cardboard box

Directions:

1. Tape a craft stick to the back of a character.
2. Make a puppet theater from a cardboard box.
3. Let students act out stories they have read, plays they have written, or use the puppets to role play solutions to conflicts.

Picture Frames

Materials:
- Bulletin board accents with writing space
- Poster board
- Tape

Directions:
1. Glue a photo or drawing to the center of a bulletin board accent.
2. Cut a triangle from poster board approximately 4" tall and $2\frac{1}{2}$" across at the base.
3. Tape the triangle to the back of the accent, so it stands out straight behind the accent.
4. Prop up the accent using the triangle as a stand.

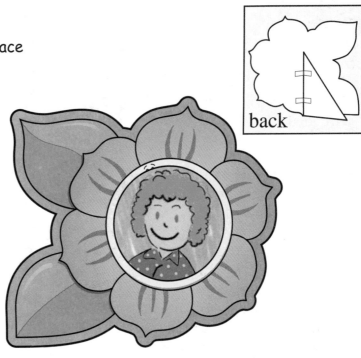

back

Ornaments

Materials:
- Seasonal bulletin board accents
- Hole punch
- Ribbon
- Glitter, buttons, ricrac, etc.
- Glue

Directions:
1. Let students decorate bulletin board accents with glitter, ricrac, sequins, etc.
2. Punch a hole at the top of each accent.
3. Thread ribbon through the hole and tie in a loop.
4. Hang the ornaments on a tree or bulletin board.

Feltboard Pieces

Materials:
- Assorted bulletin board accents
- Felt
- Rubber cement
- Felt board

Directions:
1. Brush rubber cement on the back of an accent and adhere to a piece of felt.
2. When dry, cut off the excess felt around the accent.
3. Press the accents onto a feltboard.
4. Let students manipulate the accents to dramatize a story, work out a math problem, or create a display.

back

Mobiles

Materials:
- Coordinating bulletin board accents
- Hole punch
- Thread
- Hanger
- Permanent markers

Directions:
1. Bend a hanger into a circle with the hook upright in the center. See picture.
2. Punch holes in the tops of five or more bulletin board accents. If desired, write words on them with permanent marker.
3. Tie varying lengths of thread through the holes in the accents.
4. Tie the threads around the hanger with the longest in the center.
5. Hang the mobiles by the hanger hooks.

Wreath

Materials:
- 12 bulletin board accent pieces (accents that are roundish in shape work best — you may also combine coordinating patterns)
- Poster board
- Glue
- Ruler or large compass
- Scissors

Directions:
1. Cut a ring from the poster board, 9" in diameter in the inside, and 12" in diameter on the outside.
2. Arrange the accent pieces around the ring, overlapping as necessary.
3. Glue the pieces to the ring as arranged.
4. Add a bow, a mini accent piece, or a cluster of accent pieces to the bottom or to one side, if desired.
5. Display the wreath on a classroom door, window, bulletin board, or on the front of the teacher's desk!

Playing Cards

Materials:

- Index cards
- Assorted stickers in four different designs

Directions:

1. Adhere stickers to index cards in groups of one to eight. Create four suits of cards by making sets from one to eight for each sticker design.
2. Let students use the cards to play simple games such as *Go Fish*, *Crazy Eights*, or *Concentration*.

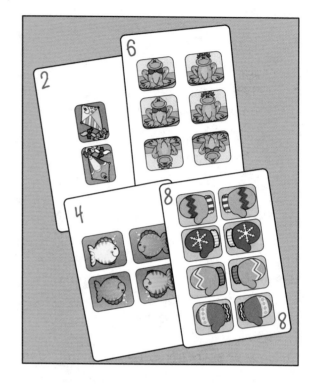

Path Game Boards

Materials:

- Poster board
- A variety of stickers
- Die
- Game pieces
- Pen or marker

Directions:

1. Create a game by placing a pathway of stickers across the poster board.
2. Mark the first sticker *Start* and the last sticker *Finish*.
3. To make the game more challenging, mark several stickers with phrases like *Move ahead two spaces*, *Lose a turn*, *Move back one space*, or *Roll again*.
4. To play the game, have students roll a die, then move the appropriate number of spaces. The first player to reach *Finish* is the winner.

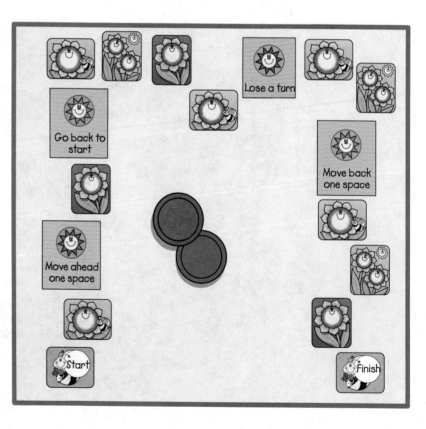

File Folder Games

Materials:
- 2 file folders
- Assorted stickers
- Pens or markers
- Scissors

Directions:
1. Open the file folder. Program the folder with skills, such as addition or multiplication facts.
2. Adhere stickers to another file folder and cut them out. Program them with the answers.
3. To play, have students place the answer stickers next to the problems.

Lotto

Materials:
- Two to four 6" x 6" poster board squares
- Assorted stickers
- Poster board scraps
- Scissors

Directions:
1. Divide the poster board squares into nine 2" sections. Place a different sticker in each section. Place different combinations of stickers on each grid.
2. Create game markers by attaching the same sticker designs used on the grids to poster board scraps. Cut out the pieces.
3. Place the game markers in a container.
4. Let the players take turns choosing a game marker from the container. If the player has the chosen stickers, she covers the picture on her grid using the game marker. If she does not have the sticker, she returns it to the container. The first player to completely cover her grid is the winner.

Stickers

Dot-to-Dot Pictures

Materials:

- Assorted chart seals or small circle-shaped stickers
- White paper
- Markers or pens
- Pencils

Directions:

1. Have students lightly sketch simple pictures on paper.
2. Provide chart seals or small stickers and have students place them on their pictures. Let students use pens or markers to number the stickers appropriately to create dot-to-dot pictures.
3. Have students erase the pencil lines on the pictures.
4. Allow each student to trade her picture with a partner, then connect the dots to complete the picture.

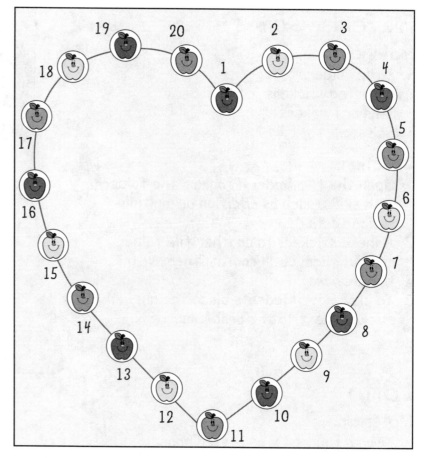

Charades Cards

Materials:

- Assorted animal stickers
- Index cards

Directions:

1. Make game cards by placing an animal sticker on each index card.
2. Place the cards in a container.
3. Let each player choose a card and act like the animal pictured, while the other students guess the animal.

Gift Bags

Materials:

- Lunch bags
- Assorted thematic or holiday stickers
- Colorful markers

Directions:

1. Give each student a lunch bag.
2. Have students decorate the lunch bags for a holiday or special occasion using the stickers.
3. Let students add personal messages using colorful markers.

Jewelry

Materials:

- Assorted shape and square stickers
- Poster board
- Scissors
- String
- Hole punch
- Stapler

Directions:

1. Create necklaces by placing shape stickers on poster board and cutting them out. Punch a small hole in the top and thread a length of string through. Tie the ends together.
2. Create bracelets by attaching stickers to a poster board strip. Size to fit a student's wrist, then staple the ends together.

Stickers

Stick Puppets

Materials:

- Square stickers picturing characters or animals
- Wooden craft sticks

Directions:

1. Attach a sticker to the top of the craft stick.
2. Turn the stick over and attach a matching sticker to the back of the first sticker.
3. Let students use the puppets to act out stories.

Personalized Pencil Boxes

Materials:

- Small box
- Assorted stickers
- Markers or pens

Directions:

1. Give each student a small box in which to store school supplies.
2. Let students personalize their boxes using stickers. Have them write phrases such as *My favorite animal is…, My favorite color is…,* and *My favorite holiday is…,* then attach stickers to answer the questions.

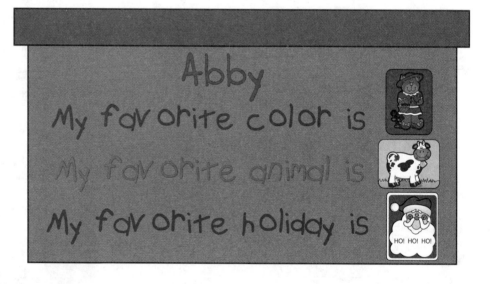

Big Board Games

Materials:

- Large and small note pads of the same design
- Large piece of poster board
- Markers
- Stickers

Directions:

1. Create a game board by attaching large note pads to the poster board. Label the beginning of the game *Start* and the end of the game *Finish*.
2. Create game cards by writing questions on small note pad pages.
3. Make game pieces by adhering stickers to poster board. Then, cut them out. Number the stickers to designate players.
4. To play, have students take turns choosing cards and answering the questions. The first person to reach *Finish* is the winner.

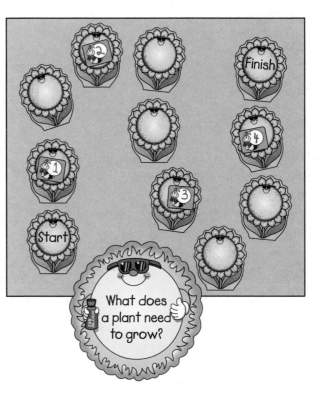

Two-Piece Puzzles

Materials:

- Large note pad
- Scissors
- Marker

Directions:

1. Cut a large note pad sheet in half.
2. Program half the sheet with a math problem, part of a compound word, etc.
3. Write the answer to the problem on the second part of the note pad page.
4. Place the pieces in a bag or container. Have students complete the puzzles by correctly matching the two pieces.
5. For older students, use different note pad designs for the puzzles. For younger students, use the same note pad design for the puzzles.

Gift Tags

Materials:

- Large note pad
- Marker
- Hole punch
- Ribbon

Directions:

1. Write a personal message on the note pad.
2. Attach the note pad to a gift by punching a hole in the top and threading a length of ribbon through the hole. Tie the ends together.

Draw a Design

Materials:

- Large note pad
- Paper
- Glue
- Pencil
- Crayons or markers
- Scissors

Directions:

1. Cut the note pad page in half.
2. Glue one half of the note pad to the paper.
3. Have students draw and color the other half of the design.

"Stuffed" Animals

Materials:
- Pages of a large note pad featuring an animal or character
- Cotton balls
- Stapler

Directions:
1. Staple two pages of the same note pad design together front to back leaving a small opening.
2. Stuff cotton balls inside. Staple the opening closed.
3. Use the stuffed animals as classroom decorations.

Picture Frame

Materials:
- Large square- or rectangle-shaped note pad with border
- 4" x 6" photograph or drawing
- Craft knife

Directions:
1. Place a photograph or drawing on the note pad.
2. Use a craft knife to make a small slit where each corner of the photograph or drawing will be.
3. Slide the corners of the picture into the slits to create a frame.

Hopscotch

Materials:
- Punch-out numbers
- Masking tape
- Clear packing tape
- Small stone

Directions:
1. Use masking tape to make a hopscotch game on the floor.
2. Use clear packing tape to attach the punch-out numbers inside the hopscotch game.
3. Let students play the game by tossing a stone on the board, then hopping to the place where the stone landed.

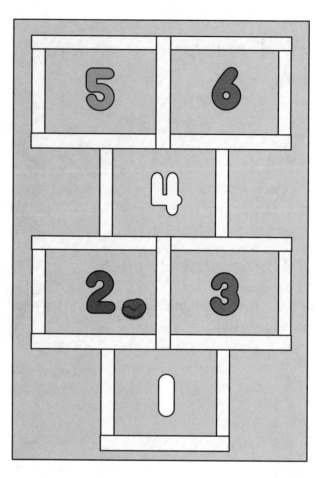

Stencils

Materials:
- Punch-out letters and numbers
- Paper
- Pencil
- Crayons and markers

Directions:
1. Punch out the letters and numbers.
2. Let students trace the numbers and letters to make stencils.
3. Students can also trace the templates to make stencils.
4. Provide crayons and markers for students to color their letters and numbers.

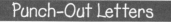

Pick a Letter Game

Materials:
- Punch-out letters
- Bag or container
- Paper
- Scissors
- Glue

Directions:
1. Place an assortment of punch-out letters in a bag or container.
2. Have each student pick a letter from the bag.
3. Have him draw and cut out pictures of objects beginning with the letter.
4. Let students glue their pictures to the punch-out letter.
5. Younger students can cut out and glue magazine pictures to the punch-out letters. Older students can write words with the appropriate initial consonant on the punch-out letters.

Toss and Spell Game

Materials:
- Punch-out letters
- Bean bag

Directions:
1. Place a group of punch-out letters on the floor.
2. Have students spell words by tossing a bean bag on each letter.

Punch-Out Letters

Comic Strips

Materials:
- Border strips
  (scenes with people, animals, or characters doing something work best)
- Plain paper
- Pens or markers
- Scissors
- Glue

Directions:
1. Give each child a section of border containing two or more characters.
2. Instruct children to write something on the border for each character to say or think.
3. Have each student draw speech and thought balloons on the plain paper and write the characters' thoughts and phrases inside the balloons.
4. Cut out the speech balloons and glue them to the border strips beside the appropriate characters.
5. Display the "comic strips" on a bulletin board.

Story Starters

Materials:
- Border strips (scenes with people, animals, or characters doing something work best)
- Large container or bag
- Writing paper
- Pencils
- Scissors

Directions:
1. Cut several different border strips into sections and place in the container or bag.
2. Let each student choose a section from the container.
3. Have students write stories based on the scenes and characters on their borders.
4. Display the border sections on a bulletin board.
5. Let each student read his story. Challenge the class to guess which border was the inspiration for his story.

Story Covers

Materials:
- Scalloped border strips
- Large construction paper
- Scissors
- Ruler
- Glue or rubber cement

Directions:
1. Fold the two ends of the construction paper in, leaving a 2" space in the middle.
2. Match up two scalloped borders so that they mesh together, and place them along the middle of the folded paper.
3. Glue the borders to the paper so one border is attached to the right folded section and one is attached to the left folded section.
4. Trim off the tops and bottoms of the borders to match the size of the paper.
5. Open the two sides and write or staple a story inside.

Pocket Chart Cards

Materials:
- Assorted border strips
- Scissors
- Pocket chart

Directions:
1. Cut border strips into individual picture squares and 8" strips.
2. On the backs of the strips, write the word that tells what is in the matching picture square.
3. Place the words and picture squares in a pocket chart.
4. Have students sort the cards, matching the words to the pictures.
5. Students can self-check by looking on the backs of the word cards to see that the patterns match the picture cards.

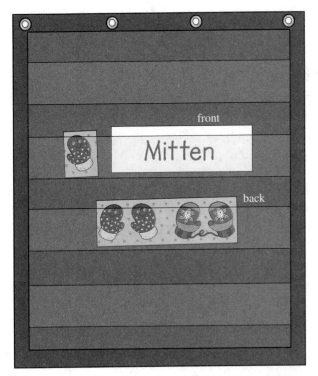

Readers' Helpers

Materials:

- Straight border strips
- Colored acetate (available at craft stores) or clear acetate colored with a highlighter
- Scissors
- Ruler
- Rubber cement

Directions:

1. Cut a 12" section of straight border.
2. Cut a $1/2$" x 12" piece of colored acetate.
3. Use the rubber cement to glue the acetate strip to the back of the border section so that a little more than $1/4$" of the acetate shows above the top of the border.
4. As students read, let them place their readers' helpers over the text so that the colored acetate highlights one line at a time.

Accordion Books

Materials:

- Straight border strips with a scene
- Glue
- Permanent marker

Directions:

1. Accordion fold a strip of border, breaking up the scene into relatively equal sections. Try to get whole pictures in each section.
2. Put glue on the back of each section, except the last, and press the accordion folds together, forming pages with pictures on both sides.
3. Let students write stories based on the pictures to go in the book.
4. Write the appropriate text on each page and a title on the front.

glue

On The Pond

by Sarah Patterson

Greater Than and Less Than

Materials:
- Border strips with countable objects
- Scissors
- Large plain paper
- Markers
- Glue

Directions:
1. Cut border strips into sections that picture different numbers of objects.
2. Glue the sections beside each other on a sheet of paper, leaving a space between them.
3. Let students count the objects in each section, and then write a greater than or less than symbol in between.

Nonstandard Measurement

Materials:
- Straight border strips with a pattern of regularly spaced objects
- Paper and pencils

Directions:
1. Provide each student with a strip of border.
2. Model how to measure using the pattern on the strip. For example, if the border strip has bees across it, you may measure your hand as *about two bees long.*
3. Give students a list of objects around the room (including themselves) to measure with their "rulers."

47

Number Line

Materials:

- Border strips with a pattern of regularly spaced objects
- Permanent markers

Directions:

1. Give each child a strip of border.
2. Have students number the objects on the borders from left to right, starting at zero.
3. Show students how to solve a problem by counting up and down the number line, pointing to the numbers as the problem is called out.
4. Call out math problems, such as 3+4-2+1=?

Bar Graph

Materials:

- Assorted straight border strips
- Glue or rubber cement
- Butcher paper
- Markers
- Scissors

Directions:

1. Draw and label axes for a bar graph on a large piece of butcher paper.
2. Place strips of border vertically along the bottom axis and draw a line on the border where the bar needs to be cut.
3. Cut the border to the desired length and glue to the paper.

Fraction Bars

Materials:
- Matching straight border strips
- Scissors
- Ruler
- Permanent markers

Directions:
1. Cut one strip of border into halves, one into thirds, and one into fourths.
2. Label the pieces of border on the backs with the appropriate fractions and label the back of a whole strip as *1 whole*.
3. Place the strips at a math center and let students piece together the correct fractions to create a whole.
4. Let students refer to the whole strip for reference and check their answers by looking on the backs of the pieces.
5. If desired, post questions at the center. Questions might include *How many different combinations can you find to equal one whole?* or *How many fourths equal one half?*

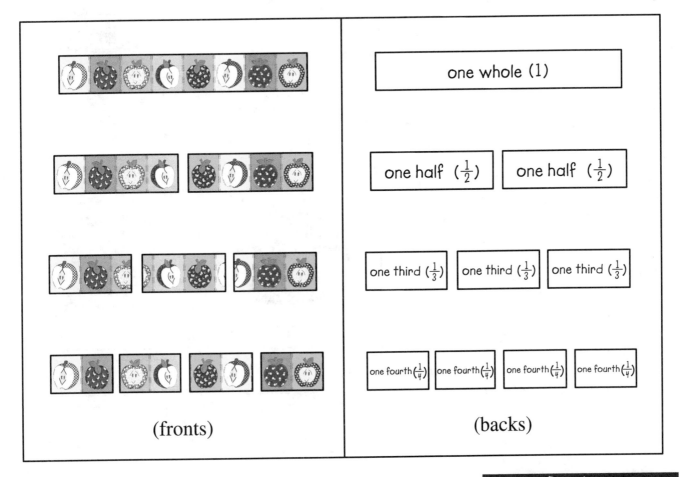

(fronts)

one whole (1)

one half ($\frac{1}{2}$)   one half ($\frac{1}{2}$)

one third ($\frac{1}{3}$)   one third ($\frac{1}{3}$)   one third ($\frac{1}{3}$)

one fourth ($\frac{1}{4}$) one fourth ($\frac{1}{4}$) one fourth ($\frac{1}{4}$) one fourth ($\frac{1}{4}$)

(backs)

Borders

Word Wand Pointer

Materials:
- Bulletin board accents
- Cardboard
- Scissors
- Glue

Directions:
1. Cut a 20" x 2" strip of cardboard.
2. Glue a bulletin board accent to the end of the cardboard strip.
3. When reading a big book or completing a class pocket chart activity, let students take turns holding the word wand and pointing to each word as it is read.

Word Wall Letters

Materials:
- 26 bulletin board accents with writing space in the center
- Permanent marker
- Index cards
- Masking tape

Directions:
1. Write each letter of the alphabet on a bulletin board accent.
2. On a classroom wall, evenly space out the accents in alphabetical order.
3. Write high frequency, holiday, or vocabulary words on index cards or sections of sentence strips and tape them under the appropriate letters on the wall.
4. Let students refer to the wall during language arts activities.

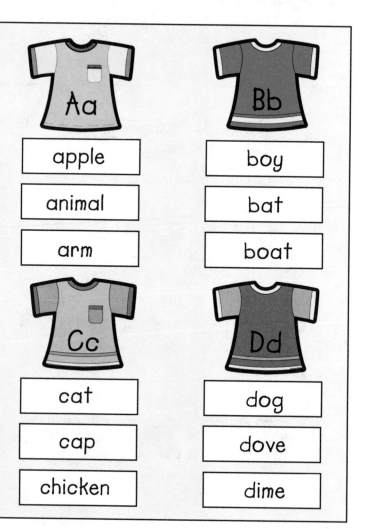

Shape Books

Materials:

- Assorted bulletin board accents
- Lined or plain paper
- Poster board
- Scissors
- Pencil
- Stapler

Directions:

1. Trace a bulletin board accent on poster board and cut it out.
2. Trace the accent on writing paper and cut it out. If using lined paper, lines should be oriented correctly for writing.
3. Place the lined paper in a stack behind the accent and place the poster board cut-out behind the paper.
4. Staple together along the top or left side.
5. Let students write stories inside the accent shapes and write titles on the covers.

My Trip to the Dentist

Manipulatives for Story Problems

Materials:

- Assorted bulletin board accents
- Paper
- Pencil

Directions:

1. Write word problems about objects pictured on bulletin board accents.
2. Place the word problems and bulletin board accents at a math center.
3. Let students work out the problems by adding, subtracting, grouping, etc., the manipulatives to find the answers.

Nancy decorated 5 eggs, but broke 1. How many eggs does she have left?

Bulletin Board Accents

Ordinal Numbers

Materials:
- A set of bulletin board accents that face in the same direction
- Permanent marker

Directions:
1. Write ordinal words and/or numbers on accent pieces.
2. Mix them up and let students order them from left to right in a pocket chart or along a chalkboard tray.

Number Display

Materials:
- 10 different sets of bulletin board accents
- Butcher paper
- Glue
- Marker

Directions:
1. Write the numbers 1-10 down the left side of a sheet of butcher paper.
2. Beside each number, glue that number of bulletin board accents. For example: one smiley face, two shoes, three children, four books, etc.
3. Display the chart as a pictorial reference for students.

Place Value

Materials:

- Assorted bulletin board accents with open writing space
- Permanent marker

Directions:

1. Give each student a set of bulletin board accents, numbered 0-9.
2. Call out directions for placing the numbers in order according to place value. For example, *Put 2 in the hundreds place, 4 in the ones place and 6 in the tens place.*
3. Then, have students tell what number they have made.
4. During the activity, the teacher should circulate around the classroom to easily check the cards for correct and incorrect answers.

Flash Cards

Materials:

- Assorted bulletin board accents
- Permanent marker

Directions:

1. Write basic math problems on the fronts of bulletin board accents.
2. Write the answers to the problems on the backs of the accents.
3. Let students take turns quizzing each other on the facts.

Number Guessing Game

Materials:
- Assorted bulletin board accents with open writing space
- Permanent marker

Directions:
1. Write a different number on each bulletin board accent.
2. Place the numbered pieces in a box, hat, or bag, and place a chair at the front of the classroom.
3. Ask a student volunteer to sit in the chair, facing the class, and choose an accent from the box without looking at it.
4. Instruct the student to hold up the accent so the class can see it, but he cannot.
5. Have the student ask the class *yes* or *no* questions about the number on the accent he is holding. For example, *Is the number even? Is the number greater than ten? Is the number a multiple of 4?*
6. Allow the student to ask ten questions. If he correctly guesses the number, he gets to choose another number and play again. If not, another child gets a turn.

Stationery

Materials:
- Blank sheets of paper
- Assorted stickers
- Pencils
- Markers

Directions:
1. Have students choose stickers and use them to create a border around the paper.
2. Encourage students to use the stationery to write letters or send special greetings.

Rebus Stories

Materials:
- Sentence strips
- Assorted stickers
- Pencils

Directions:
1. Have students choose a variety of stickers.
2. Let students think of sentences or a story they can write using the stickers in place of words.
3. Have students write their stories or sentences on sentence strips, placing the stickers in the place of words when appropriate.

55

Stickers

Patterning

Materials:

- Several sets of stickers of the same design
- Sentence strips

Directions:

1. Use the stickers to begin a pattern at the left side of a sentence strip. For younger students, complete the pattern two times.
2. Provide additional stickers and let students continue the pattern on the sentence strip.

Picture Math Problems

Materials:

- Stickers
- Index cards
- Paper
- Pencil

Directions:

1. Use stickers to create addition and subtraction problems on index cards.
2. Place the index cards at a math center and let students write and solve the problems.

Marking Vertices

Materials:

- Paper
- Chart seals or other small stickers
- Pencil

Directions:

1. Have students use stickers to make shape outlines, placing the stickers at the vertices of the shapes.
2. Let each student trade papers with a partner.
3. Have the partners draw lines between the stickers to make the shape. Challenge them to identify the shapes they make.

Stickers

Invitations

Materials:
- Large note pads
- Marker or pen

Directions:
1. Choose a note pad that relates to your party or get-together theme.
2. Write important information, such as date, time, and place on note pad sheets and use them as invitations.

Word Family Pull Cards

Materials:
- Large note pad
- Strip of paper
- Craft knife
- Pen

Directions:
1. Choose a note pad that depicts something that corresponds with a word ending the students are learning.
2. Write the word ending in the center of the note pad page.
3. Use a craft knife to make a slit at the top and bottom of the note pad page.
4. Size a paper strip to fit into the slits.
5. Write the initial letter or letters on the strip.
6. Slide the strip into the slits. Let students move the strip to create new words.

Book Nameplates

Materials:
- Small note pad
- Rubber cement
- Markers

Directions:
1. Let students choose a small note pad page to use as a book name plate.
2. On the note pad, have students write their names and classroom number.
3. Attach the nameplate to the inside cover of the book using rubber cement.

Classroom Labels

Materials:
- Large note pads
- Marker

Directions:
1. Find objects around the classroom whose names students are learning.
2. Write the name of each object on a note pad page.
3. Display the labels above or near classroom objects to encourage word recognition and print awareness.

Note Pads

Story or Poem Writing

Materials:

- Large note pad
- Pencils
- Markers

Directions:

1. Have students choose a note pad about which to write a story or poem.
2. Let students write their stories or poems on the note pad pages, then add illustrations using markers.

Bees make honey. The honey is kept inside the beehive.

Group Graphing

Materials:

- Sheet from a large note pad
- Piece of chart paper
- Tape
- Pencils

Directions:

1. Give each student a sheet of note pad paper and have him write his name on it.
2. Laminate the note pad pages.
3. Draw a large graph on a piece of chart paper.
4. Let students use tape to attach their note pad pages to the class graph.
5. Save the note pads to use with class graphs throughout the year.

What flavor ice cream do you like?

| Jack |
Tom		Midge
Stan	Jan	Larry
chocolate	vanilla	strawberry